Create And Launch Digital Products Online Step By Step

SADANAND PUJARI

Published by SADANAND PUJARI, 2023.

Table of Contents

Copyright

Copyright © 2023 by **SADANAND PUJARI**

Create And Launch Digital Products Online Step By Step

First Edition: Dec 2023

Book Design by **SADANAND PUJARI**

About

Ready to take control of your income and create a steady stream of revenue through digital products?

Look no further!

Unlock the Potential of Digital Product Creation: Launch a Profitable Venture Today!

In this comprehensive Book, you'll learn the step-by-step process of creating and launching successful digital products.

From music to chapters, and ebooks to online Books, digital products have become a popular and convenient way for entrepreneurs to build their businesses and generate income.

But what makes a digital product profitable?

And how do you even create one?

Our Book includes three parts to ensure your success: Building digital products from a strategic perspective, a technical chapter where we will work together to create your first digital product, and an introduction to powerful copywriting, essential for any product's success.

You'll learn how to identify a trending niche, build an effective product step-by-step, and leverage the secret formula of success and free resources at your disposal.

You'll also master the art of writing powerful product descriptions and gain hands-on experience creating your first digital product.

So what are you waiting for?

Whether you're a stay-at-home parent, a digital entrepreneur, or simply looking for new business opportunities, this Book has everything you need to launch a profitable venture. Join us now and take your first step toward a brighter financial future!

Take Action NOW!!!

The Start

Hello, everyone, and thank you so much for taking this instant launch challenge. This is the challenge we are facing. You are going to launch your product in nine days, within 30 hours, a span of time. And here I am going to be helping you hand holding you creating your first product. Now, let me tell you what is the logic behind, you know, creating this product. See, I told you the story.

The story of mine is when I was about to launch my product, it was, you know, I was mentored by many people. I was lost in a lot of the information. And it was taking too much of the time. The game plan was for 90 days and three days of investment. And a lot of your time, that has to be taken there. And ultimately, it took me three months, six months, 12 months to launch my product. And I failed miserably, miserably, failed to create my product and launch it because it was digging too much of the time, too much effort, too much technical knowledge I had to gain. And that's why I almost gave up.

I had finally won. I had a lot of little things I learned there. And I thought, you know, whatever was my second product, that was my upswell. I thought, why not create this? You know, why not launch this up? Tilbrook. My front end product was not ready yet. My front end BORTAC was my one Book. That is an expert positioning blueprint. That was on my front door, but it was taking too much of the time and is still there in Mahadi. So I'm working on it, but it took a lot of time. So I launched this lifetime content. This was like God, this was created by a popular product. I made all the necessary things.

So I was there. And when I launched that, I did not know it would work. It was not a Book, by the way. It was not, Of course. So it did a miracle there. In the first mundanely, we generated more than one like rupees. And that was crazy for me. Like if I tell you the revenue during that time and the profit out of it, forget about the revenue property. Pro profit was around 60 to 70 thousand rupees. So we did very well after that. There were some issues.

So we had to stop that product. But again, when I launched in December, I remember I was out for my wedding anniversary, and that time I was not able to work on the product. And three days in three days itself, it had generated me 45000 rupees.

When I came back on Monday, I saw the message that in my bank account forty five thousand rupees were delivered. And I was shocked. So this made things very, very different for me. And then I really just focused on this. And I realized that the big problem for me was I was taking too much of the time to create the product. And there I did one thing. I launched many other products as well. And this story is this. Gísli, I'm going to show you Timan again in the Book of this launch period. OK, but before that, I want you to do a few things, OK? We will be before jumping to the pro to the Book, to the launch itself.

I want you to go through the seven sutras that I followed to create your product, OK? Are not two big things. A small sutra that you can walk upon, OK, but they are going to give you a lot of reasons. They are the things that change the mindset, right? Yeah. So these are the seven who trust what you should be doing before that. Remember, before starting this challenge, I want you to always keep yourself ready with the pen in paper all day, if possible. Just get one degree for yourself. Please do that. That is going to really help you a lot. No, it's in the Seven Sutra that what we are going to do is the first thing. Is that your goal? I want you to set your goal. And in first three months,

First three months, you can set your goal. Exact number. In the first three months, I want to generate one Leko billion profit. I'm not talking about revenue but rather profit. So in the first three months of launching your product, you have to create or your 200 minimum one like rupees in the profit you can the maximum whatever number that you want. So in the three months now, second, you go to a form that you have to write down for your formation. If you have got a diary in the diary, the first page will be writing your goods. In the first three months I am creating or I want to generate, I am generating three one like rupees or profit in the next one year. I have generated 10 like rupees, appropriate or more than that.

Whatever you like, the number that you like, you can see. And according to you, accordingly, you will have to scale it up. Then you write that the formation of automation could be a simpler one, right? You can see that I am your name generating this much profit with helping people with my mentorship program or the product that I'm creating. OK, this is the kind of information that you should be using. I'll be giving the proper template to you below so you can use Natale's self motivation. See, in this journey together, I want you to be motivated all the time, because this is very, very important, OK? And for that one thing that I learned myself from my mentors is that Rustica and that I want it to pass on to you. That is, you have to have some self motivation thing.

And for that, you can use all tangles. Or Nightingale was a very famous, you know, motivator. I was a radio worker during that time. And he has given one fabulous speech, a fabulous record that is called The Strangest Secret of the World. It is available on YouTube in Hindi, as well as in English words. And I will be giving you a link to that as well, please, every day in these nine days of the journey before you start working. I want you to hear that, OK? Even if for the time you're sleeping or before you wake, you know, after you wake up during those times, you can listen to this 30 minutes record, 30 minutes audio.

And this is going to do a lot of a lot of this is going to boost your energy boost, boost your self-confidence and give you motivation that is required to go ahead. And the next sutra is imperfect action. I don't see the only one thing if you can take away from my calls. If you ask me that, then I'll be telling you the imperfect action. Don't wait for perfection. You're not perfecting up. And perfect cause will be the perfect product will be there. And you will know you have to start with the imperfection, but you have to keep on improving it. So take imperfect Matsue action constantly. That is going to help you a lot, OK? That is also true. I don't worry that if you have not done this thing right, don't worry. Just move ahead. OK, keep on going. Good.

Keep on moving. That is what is important. Now, the next thing is these nine days, these 30 hours of the journey together. I want you to block your time every day. I would want two hours of yours, OK? Not to just give you the Book content, but to work on that, OK? So whatever I tell you, you have to work on this. So in these nine days, you will be spending most of the days, like most of the days, you will be spending only two hours on working on the things that I tell you. But there will be days like day four or five, six days 78, OK, where you will be spending more time, like five hours each day, only four days. You will have to spend four or five hours with me. OK, the rest of the days you can only spend two hours with me means you will be working on the things that I tell you.

My Book is not that like five hours of the content available to you. But yeah, so there will be some cases where you will have to work like that, OK? And these are simple things. You just have to follow what I say and you will be done with it. OK, so you have to spend 30 hours of the time in the next nine days. Of course, if there is a problem, you want to take a break in between. You can take a break and the next day you call it nine to nine days. What I'm saying, nine days are the product. United is I'm not talking about the nine days where you take the gap and all, OK? So, Of course, if you start on one and you on some for some reason on the fourth, fifth and sixth, you are a break.

So start from seven, but from seven, eight, nine, 10, 11, 12. So these are the nine days I will be considering. Okay, this nine day journey, whenever you do the Book, that is the ninth day that I'm asking you for. And for that, I want you to block your time.

Okay, so seven to nine. O'clock in the evening. Whatever side hustle time that you have, whatever time that you can block for it. Please block it and do it in your calendar. Please do it in your calendar. Then only it will be possible. Otherwise, there is a lot of noise going on and that I don't want you to happen. And remember, this is not informational calls where I just tell you the concept and then I will be setting you up sulcus where I tell you the real, real how to do it.

Things OK, not here. This is the transportational code, Of course, where I will be telling you how to do this as well. Right? I'm not going to just leave you blank with the concept. No. So please block your time to work on the things that I tell you, OK? No. Once you block the time, there will be a daily checklist. Daily techniques like everyone in my chapter have some action OK to do, and you have to maintain the daily checklist of what you want and what was on the checklist. You know, take the note and also see that whatever was told to you, have you done that? If not, if anything is left from earlier today, please complete that, OK? That is the sutra to go ahead. And finally, constant improvement. So when this is done, constantly improve it. No need to worry. No need to think about a lot of things.

I'm using the simplest technique that is possible in the market today to launch your first digital product. And these are the seven sutras I want you to follow. And remember, with the right intention, right mindset and right strategy that I'm going to tell you, you are going to be successful in this after nine days. I'm sure you are going to launch your first product. And I'm happy to see that product. I'm happy to hear about it. And I'm happy with my entire community to help you out to scale it up to the next level. Thank you so much once again, and welcome to the community. Welcome to this challenge and all the best for the challenge. Let's make your first product now in this nine. Congratulations once again.

Goal and Outcomes

Welcome, everyone. And in this chapter, we are going to talk about what are the goals that you're going to achieve? What are the outcomes that are going to happen if you take these nine days' challenge? So let me take you to the mind map where I'll be showing you exactly what I want you to get in these nine, nine days. And, you know, this Donevan will be taking the journey. So these are the results that I'm expecting that I want for you, that you should get it. So first, there will be a challenge, one challenge to challenge three, challenge four, five, six and seven, seven challenges you have to complete in the nine days. And let's first talk about the goals and outcome. OK, so the first goal is your first product will be launched in nine days. That is the first goal, OK? And it is not only a goal, it is an outcome.

I'm sure if this can be guaranteed, if you work on the same parameters on the state roadmap, you will be launching your first product in nine days, Datu, in a total of 30 hours. The second thing that you will have to do is you will launch your first ebook without writing it from scratch. How does that sound? Yeah, I'm not bluffing. I'm not saying anything, Beja, which is that you don't know that you have to put in a lot of time and then only it will be ready. I'm talking with all my, you know, presence of mind. And I'm telling you that you will be launching your first ebook without writing it from scratch. And that, too, in these nine days. The third thing, the third goal or outcome that I want you to achieve is you will launch your first Book product without me making it from scratch.

Also, in these nine days, you will start selling. You'll be starting selling the product on the ninth, the date sold and on the date. And you will be at a party in the market when you launch something. It'll be a target in the market. How you become that party once you have the e-book or something, but kind of you share the knowledge, you have some kind of program or product related to that. And then, you know, all the influence and all the influencers or whatever you are sharing the post on social media, all that comes later.

Plus, you have to have a backup product which you can offer to the market. So, yeah, these are the goals that I want you to achieve. And I'm sure if you really walk on the same parameters on the stage roadmap, you'll be achieving all these goals and they will become your outcome in nine days. And that is that I'm sure of. OK, so in the next chapter, I'll be talking about another challenge, one, two, three, four, five, six, seven, and how we have divided ourselves into different days. So you can achieve the same. Let me see you in the next chapter.

Challenge Overview

Welcome, everyone. And in this chapter, we are going to talk about what are the goals that you're going to achieve? What are the outcomes that are going to happen if you take these nine days' challenge? So let me take you to the mind map where I'll be showing you exactly what I want you to get in these nine, nine days. And, you know, this Donevan will be taking the journey. So these are the results that I'm expecting that I want for you, that you should get it. So first, there will be a challenge, one challenge to challenge three, challenge four, five, six and seven, seven challenges you have to complete in the nine days.

And let's first talk about the goals and outcome. OK, so the first goal is your first product will be launched in nine days. That is the first goal, OK? And it is not only a goal, it is an outcome. I'm sure if this can be guaranteed, if you work on the same parameters on the state roadmap, you will be launching your first product in nine days, Datu, in a total of 30 hours. The second thing that you will have to do is you will launch your first ebook without writing it from scratch. How does that sound? Yeah, I'm not bluffing. I'm not saying anything, Beja, which is that you don't know that you have to put in a lot of time and then only it will be ready. I'm talking with all my, you know, presence of mind.

And I'm telling you that you will be launching your first ebook without writing it from scratch. And that, too, in these nine days. The third thing, the third goal or outcome that I want you to achieve is you will launch your first Book product without me making it from scratch. Also, in these nine days, you will start selling. You'll be starting selling the product on the ninth, the date sold and on the date. And you will be at a party in the market when you launch something. It'll be a target in the market.

How you become that party once you have the e-book or something, but kind of you share the knowledge, you have some kind of program or product related to that. And then, you know, all the influence and all the influencers or whatever you are sharing the post on social media, all that comes later. Plus, you have to have a backup product which you can offer to the market. So, yeah, these are the goals that I want you to achieve. And I'm sure if you really walk on the same parameters on the stage roadmap, you'll be achieving all these goals and they will become your outcome in nine days. And that is that I'm sure of. OK, so in the next chapter, I'll be talking about another challenge, one, two, three, four, five, six, seven, and how we have divided ourselves into different days. So you can achieve the same. Let me see you in the next chapter.

Challenge Part 2

Welcome back, everyone. And in this chapter, we are going to talk about what were those challenges that I do tell you, So there will be seven challenges and that will be spanning to nine days or in total, you are to spend 30 hours walking on it. So, Of course, in the nine days you can decide. I'll be telling you how you have to divide the time also. And those seven challenges, if you complete, you'll be getting the required outcome that I told you initially in this, you know. Of course.

So let's jump into the mind map over here where I'll be showing you the screen and I'll tell you more about what are those? OK, so well, let's unravel the secrets that we have, right? Yeah. So the first challenge that you're going to take and don't worry, I am going to divide everything in a way so you don't have to spend so much time thinking about it, OK? And this is not a bluff. You will be making your first product in this seven with the seven challengers in this nine. So the first challenge is to select your niche. Nice selection challenge.

Talking more about it, how do you have to select the niche? How do you have to go on, you know, making your micronation all? And also, I'll be telling you some golden rules in each of the challenges and see the book. But one golden rule that applies to all of them is to take action. Do not think too much, OK? Remember, your first product is not your last product. Remember that? OK, your first product does not have to be too perfect, right? You have to launch a product and then go on, you know, scaling it up and improvising it and making it up. OK, so that is going to be our first challenge is to select a niche. The second product, the second challenge is going to be a product selection challenge. Here I'll be telling you how to select the product.

What did you hear? It's not a product making its product selection. And that I'm going to tell you. Okay, so you remember I told you that you will not be making a product from scratch. You're really not making the product from scratch. That is where a lot of time is, you know, getting guns. So I will tell you more about it. How do you select the product and work on it? The challenge number three is going to be a four step funnel mapping challenge. You have to map your finances and what is going to be your lead magnet, the first product core product, the backend product and add ons to that. So I will be doing that also. So on day one, you will be doing new selection data. You will be doing a product selection challenge. And it will be mapping out your funnel. They are just conceptual things.

You don't require a lot of work to do over here. But yeah, you're in the requital decision making process and you have to make the instant decision or you get the door to take the design and take the action are going to win. Yeah. The challenge for is, you know, among the two most important challenges of the entire, you know, this instant launch in the future. Number four, what is most important? One, because you are, you will add value to the product, you will craft your product, you will, you know, make the product your own.

You will be working on a product here a lot. So I'll give you, you know, the date four and five to two days are required. And Bordelais, you will have to work five, five hours on both days. So you can work on the value addition of the product and formalize the formula that we will be using. It is very interesting. And you are not an intrapreneur kind of formula. So that will be the day forward. And if you're OK on day six, you'll be taking the ceiling and we'll find is this product packaging ceiling? Remember, packaging is everything right to packaging will be done. How to make your product look better, how to make, you know, look and feel of the product better. That will be doing it here in the channel.

No fibbed on the basics. On day seven, we'll be doing a system setup challenge. So day seven and day it these two days, we'll be giving you more time to set up your system. No. Thirty are not 30 days, 90 days. Hedstrom set a challenge in all. You'll be doing it for only two days and I'll be making it so simple that you have to, you know, you don't have to worry about it. It's going to be that you don't require a lot of technical knowledge. Also, you know, it is going to be very easy and quick for you. Yeah. So that's what I'm going to tell you here. And then we show the next challenge with this challenge segment. We will be launching your first product on the day night. Okay.

The trade dent will be the day where you will be selling your product. So in these nine days every day, you have to give to us through the China brand to us witchell. No future. Two. Absolutely no. Three. Then in China, before you will be used to this day for a solid effort. And if we are, you will be spending five hours in both of them. They are channel number five. You will be doing on the day six or two hours are required for that day's challenge. Six will be done on day number seven. Day number eight.

Well, you will again spend the fight to fight AIDS. You know, technology in totality. And day seven, you will be launching your product. So if you see challenges one, two, three. So they are two to two hours or six hours. Then product packaging tools required and launch tools are required for a total, 10 hours to do this. And channel number four, which is a value addition in total to these antennas, are required for this and they're not required for system setup. So in total, 30 hours of your work will lead you to launching your first product. And if you like this idea, just, you know, give thumbs up from your heart and, you know, just come into this crazy, awesome. Just comment below. This is crazy, awesome. If you found it wonderful, the next chapter will be starting with the China boat one. Yeah.

Niche Selection Challenge - 3 Core Desires

Hello, everyone, and in this chapter, as I told you, will be starting number one on the day fast itself. So I will tell you how you are ready to take some pain people with you and you'll be getting an idea of. Again, I'm telling you here, you do not require a lot of thinking while you are in the decision making process. OK, decision making process, though, if that is how you're going to go in and you're going to win this battle. So let's dive into the mind map and we will be talking more about what is your first JULLIEN number first and you know how to conquer this.

So, yeah, I hope you can see me on those screens as well as me, too. So let's dive into the challenge number one, which is nice selection, chelate. So you have to select your niche. You cannot be you know, you cannot go and position yourself by spotting something which is like, you know, very broad. So let's suppose, you know, you cannot say I'm this expert, that you have to be very specific about it and your niche should be the one which you are interested in and you get some money out of it. OK, I'll tell you more about it. But yeah, so that is the very first thing that you want to decide about which Nishu to use when I'm working.

Now let's talk about this election, Joan. OK, in that first, let me tell you what. There are three core desires. Before understanding any need, you need to understand there are three core desires that make all the difference. So in this chapter, I'm going to talk more about ego desires and then we'll be talking about micro niches, selecting your target market. And there is a golden rule that is going to help you move ahead. OK, so let's talk about tricot desires. So the first desire is health. The second is wealth. And the third desire is a relationship, OK, relationship with appreciation and all that. This psychological desire. And that has changed all the gaming, the marketing as well. Okay.

Marketing and advertising business. So if you see now you made the A you may think, you know, there can be multiple desires. And this also. Yeah, there can be. But if you look at the broader level, you realize that all the needs and all the wants of the human kind can be matched up to this, you know, match industry desires like health, wealth and relationship. Of course, there can be security and all. But again, I'm telling you, too, that that also falls into either the health category, wealth category or relationship category. So now let me tell you how exactly it looks. OK, for an example. Either your product, either your product, whatever kind of product you might tell is fulfilling the desire of help, you know, getting better health, getting in better shape or related to help, or it is fulfilling the desired up, you know, making more wealth or, you know, getting rich or something like that. Or it is fulfilling the desire all for, you know, appreciation by the orders. That is kind of a relationship.

OK, so these are three design tricks that are very close to the human heart. And you have to think about what you know, what desire your product is going to fulfill. But you may have to question or doubt like, you know what, my product doesn't come in any of the three designs. That is a very different niche. Right? It has to do with the category. So, again, in the career you wear, you may find, you know, when you're talking about exactly what people want from their career, Of course, build more to it, more with more freedom, then freedom is like appreciation from the people. They get to work, though they are, you know, so they want to work and they want appreciation from the people for the work they are doing. So, again, it is full trying to fulfill the build and relationship. OK, so the angle and the perspective is going to be changing.

Well, you know, another example is usually given of the JUILLET. So now you know the Gillette rates. So can you tell me the delayed reader, this product, you know, fulfills which kind of design either it is fulfilling the desirable design or relationship design. Now, you may say, no, no, it's a beauty product. So it is not fulfilling any of the design right now. But as a marketing mind, you have to think that it is fulfilling some design and you are to link it to that. Have you seen all the advertisements of Gillette and related products? What do you notice there? You might notice one interesting thing. When they are using the Gillette product in their advertising, what are they trying to focus upon?

What are they trying to fulfill? You know, you may see there is a man who weighs in on shaving, is showing his face, and suddenly there are three or four groups of women watching him. While they're shaving, while they're shaving or something like that. So what exactly it is trying to do is trying to fulfill the desire for a relationship. Is trying to fulfill appreciation by the women to men. And this is kind of a desire that we have, we think, in the relationship. So this is the result. This product is trying to fulfill. So the same way you are to think about what design your product is trying to fulfill. If you are in finance, you are trying to teach finance. So. You are following, well, the result. If you have a business opportunity again, you are fulfilling, you know, well designed and why it is important because you need to understand how all your marketing messages you have not met.

Are you really making that you are making that accord? Is that a hit? Because I will be telling you, I will help you, you know, launch your product in the nineties and make money. So make well, OK, so wealth is the decision that I'm going to fulfill the same way you are today, whatever product you might tell, you know. But are you trying to fulfill?

Are you trying to touch that core of the desire? And if not just you, how to link that product to the core desire. Okay. I'll tell you more about it later. But yeah, these are the three desires. And when we select the micro niche or any niche, you have to understand which design you are trying to fulfill. OK, so that's it for this chapter. In the next chapter, we'll be talking more about the micro niches.

Micro Niches

Welcome back, everyone. And in this chapter, we're going to talk about the micro niches, you know, the industry and the micromanagers and just one thing, do not worry a lot about just you have to pick one industry if you're not. You know very much about my commercial, because I've seen people, you know, taking too long to decide. And I need goods. It just goes away. You know, they're not able to make the product. And that has happened also with me. So I'll be telling you more about it later on. But let's talk about what other micro niches and liquidy were in the oh, my oyo microliters.

OK, I hope you can see the mineable, you know. Yeah. So are almost, you know, 14, 15 years or you're OK, and these are the main industries under which you will have microalgae cities are just, you know, Neches and under their belt we have microliters. And the big credit for understanding the Nigerian micromanagers, I want to give it to my mentor. Always, you know, without Rustica, he has really helped me a lot in understanding nature. And Michelangelo, the problem I found was, you know, it just takes too long for the trainers or people like us, you know, to decide on modernities.

And in that entire process there will be, you know, billions more and more and more and more time to make the decision. And finally, we end up deciding nothing and making nothing. So you're Oprah product never comes under. Has that also happened to me? I found this problem happening with many people, so I thought to make the solution, not what you got.

But first, let's talk about the Micronesians, OK? So the first niche that we will use is the health fighting botnet? The second is business growth. The third is you can also call them industries. Yeah. So the help business growth make money online, career growth, personal development, soft skills, learn to speak, hobbies, spirituality, parenting, dating, survival, these survival goals, you know, it will help you if you're looking for the, you know, market which is best in us or, you know, American or European market.

So survival also, I feel, you know, of soft skills. Yeah. In India, you can do. But dating, dating and survival is really going to help you if you're looking for the international market and then finance and legal and finally freelancing. These are the, you know, broad areas, broad industries that we have. And each and every one of the, you know, industries we have micro niches. Alwiya So you can see in health, the biggest pain point of feeling about people is, you know, well, weight loss, you know, weight gain or weight loss. So let me just not add weight loss. So you can see there are many micro niches. And also we have categories so you can be all Witkin expert or weight gain for women, expert women, for men, for overweight kids, for teens.

And these Ohrid kids or teens, you know, this is going to help you a lot in the international market if you're looking for the international market. OK, you do know how to use a lot of herd over your you know, you just don't know how to use a lot of grain or you just see Benito's and I'm going to tell you, will check. Which will help you to decide, OK, so far, women for men, for overweight kids, for teens, specifically body parts, for tummy fat, bombs, and bulges in childhood. So this can make you expert in one particular niche, So you can decide anyone of this. Don't worry. I'm going to give you the Excel file of this.

You know, again, you can find it in the description, which is going to help you to decide. And, you know, not all the news is. So then other features that we have in the world, too, in the healthiest muscle building your diabetes, getting pregnant, diet, nutrition, teeth whitening, depression. Yeah, male enhancement, MetroHealth yoga, growing taller, quitting smoking, hemorrhoids, headache, anxiety, stress management addiction increases testosterone, joint pain, diabetes, cellulite removal, hair loss, insomnia, Hildegard's anger management. These again can help you a lot in the international market if you are looking for high but high blood pressure more and more Alexion diet acne quit smoking stress going vegan food allergy and healthy cooking. OK, these are the main niches over here. Do not worry.

I'm going to tell you how to select one, OK? Just go to Omniture so it gives you a better idea. OK, in the business route, you can house sales in sales. You know, lead generation Automator selling FOHN says funnel sales, chapter sales, one to one sales webinar sales, seminar sales and negotiation. This can be the areas where you can show your expertise, OK, or you can pick the niche. So in the branding conceptualisation, brand design, brand communication, brand storytelling, bench storytelling, again, can you help you a lot to get the corporate clients? You're not marketing.

You can also go into digital marketing. You can go narrower in that digital marketing, like becoming an influencer email marketing expert, social media advertising. Right, offline marketing, public relations, referral marketing and operations. You can go into project management, time tracking digital systems. You can go to the recruitment team, building efficiency in the finances. One of my, you know, friends is doing, you know, he does this us what do you call this, recruiting the right people in the organization on that. He has become an expert in that. And you're doing very well, So you can just choose one of these. Also, finance is business finance, Texas and financial system research.

And you can also do the future proofing of the industry, a new innovation in the industries. You can do manufacturing distribution. Services for franchise aggregators, you know, these are the areas where people are looking. Some knowledge, some expertise, some helpful, you know, the third one is to make money online. This is the one niche that is going to really help you. You see all the gurus in the market. Many of them are making money online, niche, you know, and niche that can help you a lot like online jobs. Here, you can be an expert to get online job blogging, business opportunities, different kinds of business opportunities right there.

And you can do digital post creation, mobile apps, sales, artificial intelligence, stock market trading. This also comes into, you know, making money. And if you tell me honestly, I will make money online, you know, that is really growing a lot. So after helping make money online is the thing. If you are looking to create your first product, then it is going to help you a lot. OK, then we have affiliate marketing, consulting, coaching, network marketing, freelancing, real estate insurance, digital business, dropship shipping, offline business investing info, product creation that I'm telling you about. Right, and the source. So, yeah, this can also help you. Career growth, career coaching, career counseling, online tutor, subject matter experts study abroad.

Admission facilitator, recruitment facilitator, one of my friends also Paul has done you know, he has become specialist. So he helps the, you know, employees to get more hike in their, you know, career from their business, from their, you know, employer. So he has become an expert in that. You can also think of some innovative ideal warriors. But right now, we don't have to think too much. I'm just telling you what to do. Plus, let us see what the career is like.

What are the different niches? You and then so many niches we have in personal development also like image building, law of attraction, mindset training, procrastination, productivity, self-awareness, body language, public speaking, goal setting, willpower and self-discipline, emotional intelligence and persuasion. So these are the different niches in personal development. Subscription is also how communication one of my mentors' roles, Bhatnagar, was started with the communication mastery. And now if you are in this industry, you might be hearing or knowing about him. And the way he is doing it is really great.

You know, I have a lot of admiration for him. So, yeah, you can do that. Also, interpersonal organization, problem solving, self-confidence, confidence is one thing I feel, you know, many people will relate to it, especially not those people who are in a career also different, those employees. So they can work too much, but they are not confident enough to show it to their employer. So, yeah, you can work on that. Also, adaptability, integrity, work ethic, leadership, work, life balance. So these are the soft skills you can work on, learn to speak it kind of playbills thing. You know, Spanish, German, French, English, Chinese, Thai, Italian, other languages can happen only if you are expert in this. You already teach this. Okay, then we have hobbies. So what to do with hobbies?

Learn how to sing, how to play guitar, how to play piano, how to play drums, wood walking survivalists, bow hunting, yoga, urban farming, our seaplanes and Dorn's Pilar's get gear cooking dance learn Chinese photography. You did learn bird girl dog food, car tricks, bow hunting, spiritualism, acoustic guitar, cricket, beekeeping, home coffee roasting. So these are two different hobbies where people would like to, you know, pay money for learning something. Spiritualities, things like astrology, hypnosis, magic numerology, paranormal psychics, religion, teret witch card tricks. These are the two different things I think people are ready to pay if you make the changes in their life, you know. So these are the different niches.

Again, parenting for toddlers. What a teenager for a special niche that is growing in India. But if you're looking for the international market niche, that is doing great in the international market. And don't worry about the international market, because I'm going to tell you about the international market, how you can, you know, launch the product in the international market, also in the dating world. This can also work for the international market for how to get girlfriend, how to get a boyfriend, how to get your ex back, how to spice up your sex life, how to spice of your life, dating advice for men, dating advice for women, how to save your relationship online dating, dating for men over 50. So these are, again, different issues, survival.

Again, this can help you in the internal market. Home defense, pipping, pipping, growing your own food, homesteading. So these are the sort of relisting finance and Léger like finance planning, tax consultant, retirement planning. I did it on Geo's export company registration, trademark registration, one of my friends. Also, you don't become specialized in the GST. So I'm doing really well. So you can also pick suchness freelancing. There are a lot of things like graphics and designing, digital marketing, writing and translation programming. And you can teach them how to make money through freelancing. I, too. This is also one of the things that you can select as your expertise or industrial real estate, business services, music and audio. OK, I'll give you the entire, you know, what you can say or acculturate of this so you don't have to worry about it.

No. Important thing is I want you to just select one of these broader areas. Do not, you know, do not use. Out of your brain, just, you know, select one of the brain areas like business growth, health, career growth, make money if you're looking to make money, then coaching, consulting, something, something, you know, just select anyone which resonates with you. I do not think too much. You know, just come up with the three ideas that I would want you to write down, three to four, you know, especially to go for three. So, one, you to select either health or business growth, make money online, any one of these three industries, first three industries and or in those three industries, let's suppose you are selected, you know, help then in health or just select, you know, like stress management or whichever you whichever you find that you would want to work in and you want to, you know, make your product.

And after that, I'm going to tell you more about it, OK? Do not you do not have to worry about your selection a lot. Just think about the three which you feel you know, you should start working on, OK? All which you feel are better off. Okay? You just have to select. So just if you are selecting the health that inhaled, you are to pick up three. If you're selecting the second, it will be busier than in business. And the third is to make money online and make money online. Just select Tanita. That's it. Do not think too much. Okay, that neither you nor you should be at least interested in this and you should be at least ready to learn about it, OK? These are the two areas that I would have for you. And just forget about everything else, OK?

Do not get involved in TUDA. You're not going all going with all the niches and, you know, getting confused about it. I've seen this happening with many gators, many Burkland years. They could not launch their product because they thought a lot about it and it gave them no results. I do not think about the authority that you do not think about the kind of knowledge that you have. Just go and pick the niches. And the next thing that I'm going to tell you is going to make you, you know, is going to just blow away your mind. OK, so just pick up those niches and you can see that I don't need a comment box.

Also below that, what is the niche that you have selected? And in the next chapter, we're going to work more on it. OK, in the worksheet, I will talk about if not just write down the Trinity or three industries and Trinitas each of them, and then we'll pick up the niches. OK, so I'll see you in the next chapter.

Understanding Target Market

Welcome back, everyone, and I hope you have done all your exercise of selecting the three industries and like three niches and three micromanagers among all of them. Now, I'm going to take you to another point of view, another perspective of, you know, selecting your niche or selecting your product creation or, you know, in which you want to create the product. So let me take you to the mind map for the year, which is going to help us better. Just a second.

And we are at Armi. I hope you can see this. Yeah. So we are at the level one challenge, one guy in the challenge when there is a nice selection or challenge, but you have to take and you have to decide which Cortazar you are opting for, which chordata you want to focus on, OK? And you cannot decide that, Of course, directly without deciding the niches. And Of course, you cannot also decide the only niches. There is one more thing that you will have to decide once you have decided and you just have one more thing you will have to decide. And this is like big industries. When they launch a product, I am going to reveal to you the secret of how a big industry launches the product. You know, the huge industries.

When you know more companies like Apple, companies like Tesla, when they launch some product, they do not just go and look, let's launch the electronica. They do not do this, They have a certain target market in their mind, you know, the customer avatar in their mind. And that is what I am going to help you today to create your customer avatar, you know, like what your customer is trying to help. The best thing I would only create, though, before creating just you know, I want you to if you have selected any niche, whatever niche you have in mind. OK, so the target market now cannot make it OK, just keep whatever niche that you have just so you don't keep that in mind and then decide what age group you are trying to focus on. Look, it's like 18 to 50 or it's like 40 to 50.

Are you focusing on your health or, you know, what are you going to do? Health weight gain or weight loss for men were about 30 or 260. So whatever age that you think is proper for your target audience that you are to. I just think that I don't age, gender, profession, geographic, common problem, common interests. OK, all this and in the age segment, just I don't. What age are you trying to focus upon if you're trying to focus on working women? Okay, so the working woman, it could be like twenty five or twenty eight to fifty. This is going to be your target market the same way you have to do. Then you have to do the gender.

It can be either male, all female or both. That is, Of course, up to you. If you are launching your product, which is related to the career, but you are focusing on the PENSO, your age group will be, Of course, 30 to 50. Right, to to to fortify. That is the age group that you are going to focus upon. So the same way you have to do the gender again, meaning male and female, the profession. Yeah. So if your product is more related, if you want to help the IT industry professional, because they can, they can be right so that you are producing the kind of propers Service-Based Profession or the business person intrapreneurs. So this has to be very clear to you all the coaches consultant like my target audience usually is from the coaches consultant to teachers, auteurs like this, kind of. So what is your target audience?

What is the profession? And this is going to help you a lot. Usually people do not. I'll tell you a golden nugget. What you're Not that is going to help you a lot. And so a lot of your money. I when I first launched my product, one of the products when I had a career setting as one of my business, and I first launched one of the products which did miserably in the industry. OK, it is, I think, way back in 2017 18. And the problem was that I was booking things on the student because my career was not near the base. It was want based, you know, they wanted it's better to have that, OK, it was a want. So people, you know, did not buy that, because one of the two reasons was, one, it was a one, because it was not necessary for them. But if they have it, it's better.

The second problem that I faced was I selected the target group or the profession, which of the students in Australia really don't have money they cannot pay. So this causes a lot of problems. You know, when you're launching your employer, especially when you are launching your info product. So what are you focusing upon? What are you targeting? That is very, very important. But if you're targeting a student like, you know, you're targeting these students or you Piers to run so it can help you otherwise, not because you don't, you don't have money to pay. And your product, though, is still one of the best products in the market. It's going to face a lot of problems, you know, in solving. But in Korea, you can do what employers can help you or if you're focusing on the students, but your target group, target audience would be parents. So parents can buy products for the student?

Well, for the children. So that can help you. And that is why you will see a lot of the Books that are focusing on the parents buying for their children. One of the examples you might have heard a lot about, you know, Vittorio's Whitehead Junior focuses on the target group being bad. Is that it? Also Service-Based parents so they can buy this product for their children. So this is what you can do. Now, the geographic location, are you trying to focus on India, in India also, which are the states that are going to be focused more upon, or are you trying to focus on the US or whatever geographic location you have?

Are you focusing on one of the atrocities or the. Traceroute is what is whatever it is, just right down the geographic location, the first countries and I know if you really are focusing on the list of possible state, different state, if you are making your product in the regional languages, then the states and then also the cities, if you are focusing upon two particular cities. But geography is very important. If you are focused, if your product is related to it in vernacular language and is only focusing upon those areas where it is already, people are aware about it. So that is geographic. Then you also have to see what are the common problems they all are focusing on.

So this also comes from the idea of uniters or Weygand problems. They have, you know, they want to gain weight or lose weight. They tell me how they want to lose weight. Okay. These are the common problems that can be. This is also a way to identify your target market and make it so simple that you have a concrete vision of whom you are going to sell the product to. OK, so you know, everything from age, gender proficient geography, the mind, when you close your eyes, you know, your ideal customers should be there in front of you, the ideal person. For one, the product is perfect. So you are not selling to others. And always remember, creating a product is not, you know, making it's not physical. So making money, creating products is still equal to serving the people. You are helping them out.

For example, I have this. You can see, oh, this is a mike. You know, someone has created this Mike. So, Of course, he has made the money. But has he helped me a lot? Yes. Help me. I am happy to pay for the money because I want to show this thing, it does so ring my need. It is helping me write the same way. There is a webcam in front of me. There is a PC in front of me. So all of them have created a product that is for sure, but they have helped create after getting the product, they help to the people who need it. So the same way you have to understand that you are solving some problem, you are helping them out. So it goes wrong if you are not targeting the wrong people.

And this happens all the time in product making, you know, and usually the people who are not into the traditional product making system, a product making process, they make this mistake. A lot of people like coaches. You know, they do not make them like they want to help people, but they do not understand the target market. So today you have to sit together, you sit and you don't discuss whatever the target market that you are focused on. Do not take too much of the time.

But just, you know, to eat a rough estimate, you know, genda probation, probation could be ideal. Some other people are on probation. It is very professional, by the way, to sell a product that has a geographic and common problem you hope to identify and then a common interest. So if let's suppose you are not in the I.T., how do you identify that he's in it? So the idea was that when, Of course, he would be interested in the Infosys company, he ought to be interested in Letitia's company. So you have to find out what the common interests are, you know, you would be interested in a little Steve Jobs apple and all that. They will be really the people who want to, you know, buy the gadgets all they want to, you know, purchase the gadgets at the very early stage. This is how you understand, too. These are the common interests of them.

What are the counters of dieting people? So you will understand languages like Java. So this is how you will target them in a beer. That is why it is very important to have a clear idea about your target market as well as your customer avatar when you do all this. There would be an ideal customer sitting there and would want your product more than you want to sell him or sell her. Are you getting this person, the ideal person, the ideal target market, the ideal customer avatar? Once you make it, you know, that person wants your product more desperately than you want to sell him or her. So that is what you have to hit them on. So, yeah, this is what you have to do. So, Neches, what I want to do that you have come up with and they are the target market. There you are to select, OK, and finally, I am going to give you the cold and your lower.

You see one thing, one mistake that I have done, and I keep on telling this all the time, that I got a lot of you know, I got lost in the, you know, the ocean of information. And that happened because of the lot of niches where there are a lot of things to do. What I know, what I don't know, what you know, I want to learn what I don't want to learn, what I'm good at, what I'm not good at. So much confusion is there. And finally, I couldn't make this one because I could not make the decision. It was too confusing. So, you know, what I would tell you to do is to select your favorite target market. Either you can be one of them. You want to be one of them.

Are you how these people are not usually related to you? So this is how you can select the target market. Secondly, just pick up Buterin issues. Whatever comes to your mind is a little bit of information. How are you going to get that information? You are passionate about it or you are interested in this particular thing. So there's two things when. Combined together. OK, then there will be some kind of niche that is there in the back of your mind. And that doesn't bode well. Don't think too much, because the golden rule is there is a trap of paralysis of analysis. So you will be analyzing too much and you will be getting into a trap of, you know, but there will be paralysis. You cannot decide anything. And remember in the book called Think and Grow Richer is one thing.

The golden age of the argument is making the decision. If we cannot make the decision. You cannot go ahead. And right now, today's important as the first challenge that I give you is just, you know, take up to three teenagers, at least, you know, whatever you are related to. And write down about your target markets. So the strangers and the target market, Of course, you're only just going to be, you know, working for the health, but for the I.T. professional, because they suit a lot of time, you know, they use their time a lot in sitting. So you want to help them out. OK, so this way. So write down your three niches, micro niches. And at one side, the other side, you have to write down your target. This is your challenge. Number one, you have to compete essentially at any cost.

Tomorrow, I'm going to tell you, how can you launch a product in the same niche or, you know, whatever niche that you have selected or even you hope you have to modify the niche, if that is the reason. And how can you make your product? How can you start making your product without, you know, starting from scratch? So just do it today and do not forget the golden rule. Do not get into the trap of paralysis or penalties, just up right down the three images and write down the target market. That's it. Do not think too much. And do not worry that your design might go wrong. And this is the one reason we are Eifel.

You know, I spent a year in Diyala thinking about, you know, this process. I could not launch the product. I'll show you sometime, you know, what product I had could not launch because of falling into all the kind of crap that I'll be telling you more about. OK, so that's it for day number one. Challenge one that you are to select on it. You are to select a target market and just write down. If you have got the idea just right on the comment box, what target market you have selected. And all the best for ceiling number one.

Remember, make this a toy today. Taking action is more important than doing anything. OK, you're taking this one is more important than doing anything. And don't worry about, you know, getting it wrong, because I'm going to tell you, either it is right or wrong. OK, so see you next. Tomorrow we'll be talking about a challenge on Matto and on day number two. OK, bye bye. See you tomorrow.

Product Selection Challenge

Welcome, everyone, and this is day two of our program here, day two of the challenge, and we are at stage number two. Let me take you to the mind map, Bill. And the challenge is to go up. You can see the mind of Mboya. Yeah. And challenges Karlberg selection. One of the most important and I will say here, because see here, I'm going to tell you the technique which can reduce your entire work from 90 percent, you know, 90 percent of the work is going to be reduced or we go and this is so important, Joan and I will want you to work on it, on the data itself.

So last we are discussing the need for selection and your target audience are the two things that you must have done and truly are on this day. Two of the challenges we will be talking about are product selection. Don't know the word here. I use this brogues selection time because there is something that is a mystery. There is magic in it. So why did I say projects of product selection challenge and what not make? Because here you don't don't know how to make the product. You have to select the product and you don't have to select, you know, someone else's product or you are to create your own product. But you have to select the private label. Right product.

Now, what is a private label like? Private label. Right, if you don't, let's suppose the private label. Is it that you get a license to use that product as your own. You get a license to use that product as your own. So what it can be, Of course it can be content can be anything. And I'll tell you more about it. But yeah, that is what many of the people have wrong, you know, ideas about the private label. But one thing I'll tell you, private label rights are, you know, private label products are very, very common. It is also known as white label products. And if you know about Wal-Mart and Wollar, Wal-Mart is one of the, you know, big franchises that uses a private label product. If you are in India, you might have seen in the demurrals, They get private label or right level products when you know someone else manufactures it and they do the branding and customization.

So the same has to be done here. But you will be doing it in a unique way, a strategic way. So it doesn't look like it's already what will make it your product. OK, don't worry about it. Let's move to the China button. And here we were talking about first you have to see you to select a product that is related to your niche. And in the process, you have to browse that product in the Biala directress or Peola platforms. OK, and there are a few player platforms that I will tell you more about. So I will be going one on one in all of those Beinert products also. So before that, I also want to tell you, BLR is kind of, you know, as if you are doing it alone, and if you are a trainer or coach or something like that, you might also know that there is a dedicated team who does the content creation part.

Right for the trainer, who does the content research. Content creation, content curation part. If you might have seen about Dr. Vivek Ben-Dror, he also has a team who works after the content creation for him, and he just presents that, OK, the same way you might have seen. So people are particular to consider pillar products the same. So there is some call to the team that is working out for you with working on the bailout product. So, Of course, it is your product only, but they are working on it. Quantitative research and everything. OK, that's the one approach to look at it, the other approaches.

Let's suppose you outsource the work of content, research, content creation to someone else. You outsource that work to someone else, like a ghostwriter, someone. And now they are giving you the final product and you have to present it. OK, it's the same. So what you have to do is everything will be done for you. There is a team, let's suppose that the team was doing it for you. OK, and you get the right to do it. So the pilot product is going to be similar for you. Okay.

You are getting the license to use it, modify it, change it, edit, customize and personalize it. OK, and we'll be talking more about those strategies also. But in the next chapter, I'm going to tell you about the different product mix and how to search for your product. You know, in these mines as well as in the other areas. OK, so yeah, that's it. Let me say in the next chapter.

Where To Get A Product From?

Welcome back, everyone. And today, we will be talking about how to select the right product for you, and we are to select it from The big question is we are to select it from three guys. I must say, you decide this is full of honesty. There are so many people you know, diked is pellagra membership site Pilla, which is full of crap. You know, all the junk has been, you know, sold over there. And I don't want that to happen with you.

You know, when you are selecting the PEOLA, it has to be a high quality premium quality product. So you can work on it. And it has to be some you know, it has to have some exclusive element. It should not be like, you know, everyone is using the same or it is available to everyone. It is available for free of cost. So that gives you an advantage of having the right property audiences. OK, so here I will be doing one thing. I'll be telling you to fight.

Honestly, I've done a lot of research. You know, I can't tell you how much time I have invested. No, you're not even looking for the right good high quality premium quality peanut products, because I've been selling it for a long period of time now. Yeah, I've done, you know, a lot of good work in this industry. A lot of you know, I've got a lot of benefit from this industry. And Of course, I use my strategies. I do not sell any product as it is. I am using my strategies. But the question here is to get the best product that is the basic product in the right format or the right quality and the premium quality. And also, you know, of the kind of premium category like high quality, OK, and there are only five to six such suppliers that will provide such a kind of product. And I'm going to tell you my secret, how I get my pillared product. And this is a really big Segretti.

You know, you'll be wasting a lot of your time if you go to the PLO, you know, membership site, and you will realize, you know, all of that is crap if you sell that in the market or ultimately you might make some money. But ultimately, Knight is not going to help you. And there will come a point of time, you know, where people who are your customer will not like the product and they will not like you, and you'll not be able to sell any kind of product. And you're not Hainsworth. So, yeah, we have to be very much cautious and the strategies that we are to use also, I'll tell you. But first, let me tell you, what are the Peola products available? Sorry.

What are the PLO membership sites available? And how can you look for them? OK, so just let me take you to mind my appeal.—. Yeah. So I hope you can see the main rebel with you and the Billah sites that we have. The top quality. Highest quality. And don't go, you know, don't go and look at any of these people, because either they are fraud, they are fake, they are scamming or they are just sites, which are you not taking product from here? And they are and use it. There are some also, you know, you may find some of them, you know, on fiber also, but do not use any Baldelli. If you are getting it, please be cautious about that, because they do not have proper licensing.

And there are so many things that we have to be careful about. You know, thinking of buying Biella broke. So they do not do that. OK, and I'll be talking more about the product pro pela license as well. Yeah. So the first or the aside that I like is Bill Adami. If you are a coach trainer or something like that, Baylor taught me is a right, you know, a membership site for your right product, you will find all the. OK, the second and one of my favorites are the most reliable. And I personally like it 80 percent of the time, even though I held an affiliate, you know, I affiliate with all of this. But you are a dohyo affiliate of one. Straubel will be allowed, you know, where I could have made more money, but I will not tell you that. I'll be telling you the secret where, you know, Of course, I will not make a dime out of it, but you will get a, you know, triple benefit from the unstoppable Pither. Okay. And that is the one site that I rely on a lot. There are multiple issues. I'll tell you more about it.

The third is the Biella sales funnel. If you are into the international Internet marketing industry, then I feel the paler sales funnel is, you know, for you and the fourth and fifth that the fourth is excluder NECHES. And this is for those people who are not able to find, you know, products related to their niche on špidla, not me, unstoppable people sales funnel so they can go and find it on exclusive niches. And then we wonder how this can cost you a little bit more, because exclusive niches are what especially not this little will cost you more because you may find some of the people that are not possible anywhere else. OK, and there is it. It is a membership site where, you know, at a very cheap price, you can get all the like 12000 products. But I wouldn't recommend this to you unless you are not able to find your product on the top three, because here in this membership site, you know, they get product from on Struwwelpeter B, a lot of were not.

And they do not give you the license, which is called parallelize. And they will give you a license, which is MMR. Emara means you can sell to others, but you can modify the license that we will be needing. ISPI Alarmist. You can private label. You can modify the content. You can modify the name and everything. OK, that's what we want here. So, yeah, one by one. I'll show you. All of them are just a second and it will be moving toward. I'll show you all the sites. So you get the idea better. OK, just sneak away. Yeah.

I hope you can see this screen. Oh, yeah. Yeah. So we are at Unstoppable Pila. That's why I told you like 80 percent of the time I use this a capella, not me. So people are not me. Is that another one that I use? I'm very willing. Your top. Not so clear skies, OK? This land of success, not and not everyone will use it in all you and your or if you do it yourself, you'll realize that you spent a lot of time, a lot of time doing this. And, you know, gone nowhere. You are just a house. You don't just waste your time. The third one is excluding Neches. OK, so I'll keep it at one, because Darwinists are balers. Salsinha, you can see the product.

All you're The photos excluding Ettus and the fifth one is IDPs. So I told you it's a membership site, right? Well, you get around a thousand products. So let me tell you first one by one about everything, OK? So if you go and search on Pela, not me, this is about the highest quality, the most premium content, if you can find anywhere that it is a pilot, not me, most reliable.

Many coaches, consultants, and Ortel use this product. OK, and what kind of product will you find here? See, now you can. I just you know, I've gone here. Let me show you. OK, this is a product category. So these are the different niches, anxiety, depression, confidence or business and marketing, career and jobs.

So if your niche is in the career, business, marketing, all your personal development, stress dating and relationship goal setting, inspirational meditation, money management, budgeting, credit debt. So this is one of the best for you. Yeah. So here is the kind of quality content that you will get. You will not get it anywhere else. OK, let's suppose. And they are Bertolaso. They are collected for you. So it becomes easier for you. Just let me show you. So, yeah, we'll be investing a little bit more. So you get all the strategies, all the important things that I use personally. Oh, Let's suppose email copywriting so you can do copywriting. But let me orthopods, it's like if you are in the sales, auto position can be helpful to you. So five products are there in this bundle.

And they will be so we will have to pay the credit and get the product. But see, this is how this e-book I think about it. So this is a rebel report, an ebook. OK, what else is included then? They have two action guides. This can be helpful if you are trying to do the workshop webinar workshop. Okay, this can be helpful. I'll tell you, the strategy is first you have to check out you know, this is like an example of the workbook or your coaching workshop. So they collected all the chapters. Yeah, this is how the chapter is ready. You have to add your flavor to it.

I'll tell you more about it. OK, now we learn the rest of the party. you know, your challenge will be well, we'll be doing, you know, value addition. So using Peola is simply, you know, when you go to the market, if you are an intrapreneur, you think this way, if you're in trouble and you're not you, you got water. So what can you do with the water? If you are an intrapreneur, what will you be able to do? You know, you will make something early. You will be mixing lemon in the water and you'll be selling it as lemon water. So one group is water. You can sell it for ten rupees. You have bad flavor.

You know, you're offered labor or something. If you do proper branding on that, you'll be selling that for 22. So that's how you have to think. OK, that's the same case with the Pela product. But there is a proper strategic deal that goes on in personalizing and, you know, walking on the bill. And I'll tell you more about it later on in the stage for the challenge. But right now, what is important for you to, you know, is select the product. I'll tell you, selection process also. But for now, just go and see what are the different or, you know, areas from where you can select the product. So this is the pilot, not me. It works on a credit basis. So you will have to pay the credit, like, see, suppose 25 credits, just this bundle, you'll get four tentacles and each credit may cost one dollar to dollar. The more credit you get, the more money you'll have to spend. OK, this is a credit based system.

Now, second is unstoppable Peola. I personally love this one because I'll tell you more here. You'll get the entire set, you know, you get. And there are two-level of the product. One is a gold product. One is the basic product. You'll be getting an e-book, you'll be getting a report, you will be getting autoresponder a little. And so much like there are, there are 10 things involved also in this . This kind of, you know, unstopping will be allowed. One of the best things I like is the gold one. You'll also get chapter tutorials. Of course, we will have to work on it. I'll tell you more about it. But you get Filiatrault tutorials and the best part is you get all the marketing materials for sales, like the sales literacies copy. You want the sales pitch and how to work on the sales pitch.

I'll tell you more about it. So my recommendation is that you go and walk more on the unstoppable and one you know, the beautiful thing I'll tell you more about more is, you know, plus just check what other products I've been able to hear. Focus, morning ritual, overcoming obstacles. So these are personal development, Instagram and digital marketing. Health related to health, social media and all this product you may find in it also. But the problem is I Repeller takes this product from this site and when they take it, they can only sell rights. So they cannot sell you Biella rights means you cannot modify the product. But if you buy it from Yale, you can modify the product and the base. Beautiful thing. I'll tell you here if you let's suppose you're not first, take out the product to sell up meditation, Of course, just to lead. OK, this is a kind of leadership boost for your online sales.

This is for the sales of peaceful kills. Traffic becomes the best version of yourself. Virtual summit. This can be for your trainer and I'll work from home. Unplug. Work from home has become very important. You know, nowadays webinars and everything is happening. It can be a good cause. You know, your first Book, the influential leader, don't worry you just how to sell it. I'll tell you how to work on it. You just have to select one of these. OK, and the interesting thing that I wanted to tell you is just, you know, let's click let me click over. Yum! OK, so this is what you'll get. It's what you should have in marketing, OK? What's included? High quality book, printable checklist, resource, structured mind map. So if you are to teach this time, a mind map is also available, So ready sales later, the sales page is available later.

Magnet, low level, high quality professional graphics are then ten quality articles. This is very important and I will tell you how to use it. Promotional email swipes social media. OK, tools, chapter tutorials 12 step by step, two tools we are training and something like that. OK, so you click here to find out more. Let me do so. Get it for thirty seven dollars. Write the first product, you get it for thirty seven dollars. And if you add them again they will sell you for the next thirty seven dollars. They will be selling you the next level product, which is, you know, gold product where you will get the chapter tutorials. OK, you want. But I would recommend taking both of them.

OK, so around it goes to around, you know, seventy eighty dollars. But I'll tell you one interesting thing that not only thirty zones within thirty dollars, you know, with thirty dollars will be getting not only one product that to go, you know, including gold. So that is like an eighty dollar product but two eighty dollars products are like one sixty dollars product. And that secret will be revealed in the next one. OK, well, should I reveal all yours only? OK, let me reveal all yours, OK? So what you have to do, you have to go here and you have to become a member. Yeah. Yes. Can you see the membership? Yeah. So you have to become a member of BLR, Unstoppable Biala. And when you become the member Soucy.

And when you become a member here among all these products, you know, this is I think. Yeah, we all have it a little lower. OK, this is I think this is not this one, the second one, the first one. OK, well, the next one was I think all the membership was available for all the products. OK, so this one I'm talking about the hundreds of the products available here, and you will be getting each month to produce. This is a monthly membership, Of course. You know, but you will be able to if you buy it, you'll be able to get it. See, twenty nine dollars a month, you'll be able to get it to produce. Are you getting the two golden products? That means around eighty and eighty dollars, like 160 dollars.

You can see from what you're not buying it for once it's a dollar. You can sell one dollar here. And let me be honest about wanting more guys. I am an affiliate of this Onestop. It would be about, you know, if I would have given you the link of the first product, I would have hundred percent of it. Right, because I am Jerricho. So I would have 100. But not if it's to your benefit here. I'll tell you about your benefit. OK, so forget about my weight, Invidia. You take the just you know, just buy it for twenty nine dollars a month. You have to just buy it for a month only because, you know, you have to start with the product. OK, and I'll tell you, because this one product can become your main product.

The other product will be your bonus product. I'll tell you more about it, how to do it. But just now, go on and search on the products of the plant, OK, whatever you like. Just, you know, pick up the one thing about it and I'll tell you more about the product selection later. OK, so yeah, but this site that you are to use the most. The third one is the Pilau sales funnel. If you are into the Internet marketing plan, and this is what I would recommend to you, OK, anything like YouTube, more marketing. And they're also famous for their making, right? Kind of the best kind of product. So your ecommerce store. Yeah, your first product. So this is also interesting. You're celebrating ultimate pursuit.

Come right to you. Anyone you can buy over here. See, we will have to do it later on. We will have to do a lot of, you know, creatively we are to work on that. But yeah, these are the three, you know, membership sites that I would recommend if you are not able to get it on these three. Still, I would recommend to buy any clothes, this one or, you know, let's suppose you're into the weight loss, OK, and you are not fine if you are into the Okay, let's suppose you are into the Cheto, So and you are not able to find any deuteride, programma, yogalates. So I would recommend you to go and search for a Dilek Tiltrotor product. OK, you are able to find it. But let's suppose if you are not So anything which is related to help, OK, that should become your first product, because I would not recommend you to go on the 4th and 5th should be your last resort, OK, when you are not finding anything, there are some like I saw, there were something related to stock market bear, which is not you will not be able to find a, you know, related to Indian stock market.

So what you have to do is to find something to invest in. Yet, Of course, here in three, you will not find it. So try to find it on the exclusionary rule to investing and also on the pillar. But I'll tell you, the problem with the boat here is I concluded it will only give you only a single ebook, OK? And that also you have to search. That should be a pilot. eBook means you can modify the content or modify the content and without pillories most of the time. So, yeah, I was searching for weight loss over here. You can see how they are given but most of the time what has happened is that they have brought this product for someone else like that and they are selling it.

So the problem here is you only get master resell rights. So it is okay to add bonuses, more and more bonuses to your main product. But I don't think, you know, the main product, the code word that we are making, we will need the product that can be modified. And here this product can not be modified. How do you understand that if you go to any one of these, let me just click on this so I'll show you how it works, you know, what other rights are given. So, yeah, you can see or whenever you click on the product, OK, this is I deplore whenever you click, click on the product, you will hear you will come to know. OK, also check the submission date. So when I know the products are new or old so you can sell the product, you can be sold for personal use, can be packaged with all products that are also good, can modify, change the sales later, sales later can be modified, OK, can be added into Pember paid membership.

OK, and you put name one, it can be offered as a bonus, can be used to build a list, can print, publish offline, can convey and sell for personal use. Can convince or resell. You can resell. Of this product. Also can convince a master estate. But what can you not do? You cannot modify it. And the main product, you cannot modify and change the graphics on Ekeler, right, so these are the two problems that we are facing. We don't want this private sale. Write down everything. We don't. We want these two, which are very important. OK, and whatever. And if you can do this, too, that means you can do the selling and all the parts of look for the you can modify and change the product name or not.

Usually Peola, if it is written Pilla, then it happens, OK? That's the problem with Node Pillar. But the benefit of the pillar is like, you know, you get four, seven thousand something, you get access to twelve thousand products, which is good if you are adding more and more one as the street. But I would recommend that as a last resort, you know, first try to get your product, you know, in this tree, but then you go for it exclusion, which is or Idella know in the next next chapter I'm going to do will use some of the strategies about, you know, selecting the product. OK, Jose, let me see you in the next chapter.

PLR Product Licenses

Yes, welcome back, everyone. And in this chapter, we will be talking more about, you know, špidla licensing. So this is one thing that is going to be very useful to you when you buy the right kind of licensing. And, you know, that is going to make the toms very clear. So let me take you to mind. We 'll be sharing you. What kind of differences are licensing? OK, so yeah, we got here to second and.

Yes, so let's talk about the different grand opera licenses. So the first license that you, you know, usually get on the pilot project is the result that you reserved the rights to the pilot product that you sell to others. This you get on it all, almost all but not on pilot, not me website. You know where I told you it is only to edit and use for yourself. Or you cannot resell the product. You can sell the product, but not resell the product. So yeah, that's one thing. You cannot resell the product as it is. So that is one thing. The second is master. All OK, Mazrui sales. Means you can resell the right to resell to anyone.

Let's suppose I'm the person. OK, I got a product from Ideology. So if I must be right to. That means I can sell the product to you. And you can also sell that product to the next person, but the next cannot. Are you getting this? I can sell this product to you and you can also sell this product to another one. So I am selling you the master resell, right? So the I how the master is all right to sell you the resell, So you can sell it to the next one. So this is how it goes. Well, but it's not too important a policy or your rebranding. This is important.

Rebranding means you can put your link in the you know, you can change the name, you can change the rebranding and everything, OK?

So that is one thing. Then let's talk about private labels, right? So not so. This is so, you know, the most important one for us in the private label. You can, you know, change the entire setup from scratch. You know, you can change everything you want from, let's say, not the content part owned article part or the chapter, but everything you can put on. So what we want is a private label, And you'll get to, you know, be lower rates like you want on the appeal or sales funnel, then unstoppable, even repeller. You will have to search and dig deeper to get the Bill of rights, But you would want Bill Rights and a pilot. Me absolutely. Give you a bill of rights. OK, so you don't have to worry about that. They give you properly, Bill. What are the bills that you can modify?

You can change the product name and change the cover and modify the cover. OK, so these are the two things. We will be seeing it and argue over the items. You can give it away for free. Some of the bills. It will not help you to know, I will not give you the license to give it away for free. But there are some that can be possible later with some product. It can be positive. But OK, so now these are the different rights that are given to you. One thing I'm again and again telling you guys that you do not buy any product, the bulk product that you get. But there are some people who sell illegally.

Those bulkiness, you know, we are, they will be giving you the difference in the huge kind of junk. And the problem with those kinds of popular, you know, products is that the licenses are sold illegally. And if you become an authority in the market and if you're selling it, you know, somebody, you may get caught, you know, and there will be a problem with it. So please do not avoid those. And again, the content that you get is very cheap. So the content is cheap. The product is cheap. And I don't want you to do that with your press product, OK? So never, ever use the cheap product Tipiloura.

Always go for high quality premium quality and the least. I've given you the Pillar product listing that is the highest of the quality Palapa that you can get in the market. OK, but in that also you have to be very specific about which product you select. Secondly, let's talk about some of the confusion you will get. You know, is it legal to get pyloric, right? The first computer? See, this is done by the big banks. You know, what we do is we outsource some kind Of course, OK, or we are getting licensed to do it. Like, you know, we're getting licensed to use that. So there is no question about it. It happens.

You know, if you are a big brand or you feel big corporate, either you will be doing it from your team, you would be either outsourcing to another agency or you are using the best product. I call it product based. So you're getting the best product and then you modify it and you're presenting it in your own way. OK, so there is no question about it. Regality. Second is whatever the corporate content. So, Of course, we will be not using corporate government and we will be working on it. We will be using our strategies. So there will be no corporate content to not worry about it. OK, but it's going to change the entire product. You will not forget about others. You will not recognize. That is what the paper product is. OK, so you'll be working on that? Totally.

People ask this question, you know, what can we use it for? You know, selling it to Amazon and everything. And I'll tell you more about it when we. For value addition. So Baylor is one of the, you know, white label, it is also called a white label industry is one of the very, you know, big industries where they work for others and they give the product owners alike. You might also have seen this happening in the auto, you know, auto industry. So there are some people, you know, who specialize in one of the basic products. So the main industry, the main interest, again, focuses the work on something else.

So like the screw and the nuts and everything right there, this other, you know, manufacturer will do that work and they'll sell it to the auto industry for a cheaper price. And that is a white label product. So they will use their brand and then they will sell it. Okay. Yeah. But the problem then, what is a problem? Why is Biella blamed for the cheap product that comes in the market? Second, a lot of illegal activity goes on. And the third isn't that a popular product is not celebrated very well, it is using it as it is. So you're getting the junkyard selling the junk, You're not working on it. You're not. That's the worst thing about our industry. And that's why we're not in the payola industry.

We are in the launch industry, or I'll be telling you how to use it, how to have it, how to use it. So you don't go away. You forget the trap of paralysis analysis. I don't know the trap of starting from scratch where you get demoralized, but you have to work so much that you get data that is not going to happen with you. OK, with districts that I tell you about. That is why people recommend that you are not using it and you are not starting from scratch. Something is built up and you are modifying it, you are personalizing it, you are contextualizing it, and then you are using it, OK, and you're upgrading it and then you are using it. S

o your first product, when it hits the market, you get that courage within you that you're going to go for the ability to generate your product. OK, so that's why Palach licenses are clear and also some of the questions and doubts that people get about the bailout. So I hope that it's clear to you in the next one, I'm going to talk to you or talk more about the product selection. How do you select the multiple products? How do you select the one? And then we'll be talking about the golden rule that is there that is so important in the. And number two. So, yeah, see you in the next challenge. In the next chapter I will be doing a real challenge. You'll get real work. Okay, so let me see in the next chapter.

Selecting the Right Product

Hello, everyone, and this is going to be the last word of the day to challenge number two, And let me dive into the mind map over here that we're talking about. How do you select the product? OK, now see, you'll have selected a niche already. You know, what is your niche, OK, or some idea about the industry. And now the next thing is you already know the different kind of, you know, a different kind of product, which is like a lot of people are not me at all. But the next thing that you're and this is really where work is involved.

OK, I have to make you. I really want you to make the decision, the decision you're making. Will you don't change the entire campaign either you will be able to do it or not. And honestly speaking, guys, you know, this is the one thing that matters a lot. I told you my story many times. You know, I was involved in product making. It took a lot of time, 90 days. I was working on the product. It took six months and then a year and could not, you know, come into reality. And one reason behind a lot of time, you know, I was not able to make the decision. There's a lot of confusion. So like but here I'm restricting your choices, OK? Either you just pick something and how.

The first thing is I want you to just whatever needs that you have in your mind. You know, take that list and all on Google, you have to browse. Let's suppose your weightlessness of weight loss, Biala, and just sit there. And if that makes you more competitive, you are not able to find the right product. What I want you to do is just go to the fight, the three or four, whatever, you know, product directory I listed, the right people are not. I do pay a lot of people our sales funnel. Unstoppable. Just go out there and find the most appropriate, you know, product that boosts your niche. OK, let's suppose if that is not your niche, okay, let's suppose there is something like, oh, OK, weight loss and in weight loss, there are many things, OK? And one thing is like fasting and on. But that's not your niche, but that's not your, you know, micronation. But anyway, if it is your niche, just take that selected product.

One thing also you have to say is how to check whether the product has a private label, right or not? OK, private label. Is very, very important for Elbaz. It should be panel based product, not based product means when you see take they understand, you know, there is a background also there is a chapter or something, you know, so that it should have like the checklist, lead magnet and everything. OK, also check that sales pages are not OK on it. You will get the sales pitch on. So there will be a lot also. You will get it or pilot it. Not me. I'm really doubtful about the sales pitch. OK, if they don't, Breugel, but this is just, you know, content creation that is done for you. So but I will start and for making your first product, The first product launch in the nineties.

I really want you to, you know, go and focus on Onestop. It will be allowed to site doctors, go there, take just such any product that you find is closest to your niche or your industry, and you are able, if you are completely brain, OK, just pick the product of your industry that you find, that you feel it's good, OK, that you would want that product for you to speak that product. OK, and do not think a lot. So that's what. Yeah, final best private label, Niche product or any blog which is closest to your niche. OK, just pick that product.

Just buy the Barberton, OK? If you're looking for the unstoppable, I would suggest you just get the membership and the golden rule. I wanna tell you here, the golden rule, which, you know, made my success delayed a year. And now I've been through a lot of trouble in that year. OK, if I would have taken one thing, if I would have done this one thing earlier than I would have been at some different place today. So the golden rule is don't reinvent the wheel, OK? Don't do the things that are already done. If you have it, just use it. And for that is to select any product from your industry, as I told you.

Right in the product selection process. So just your fill, if it's in help, just pick it up, OK? If it's healthy and weight loss, just pick it up. If it is healthy and readable again, just pick it up, OK? If it is to make money online, you're not sure. Like, you know, there are three or four products that you have in mind. Just pick the one. OK, just get the membership site and download it. Just pick the one. That's how the entire gamut. And I would suggest you like 90 percent of the time this year to go to the unstoppable pile and big product, OK? One hundredth of the products are there. And don't worry that other people will be buying the same product. Don't worry. I know how to change it.

And every month they are, you know, adding two to three products and. Various sites where you will be finding new products coming up, so don't worry, okay. It's not important what you're getting at in the, you know, the original form, right? It's important. How are you going to build your infrastructure on it? OK, yeah. The founders' foundation has to be good and solid, but we will change it. OK, will make it customized according to your needs and according to your target market. OK, so don't worry. Just pick the product and take the design. And remember, don't reinvent the wheel and select any product that you like. You're not making it and will make a lot of trouble. OK, so this is the challenge. If you have done it just in the past, just right in the comic books have done it, and just tell me what work have you selected? OK, any product can be. But yeah, go on.

Unsolvable Aperol. It will help you again. Twenty nine dollars. You can get two products. OK, so you go to that one and we'll see you better, OK? First, if you're going to Onestop ever be around. One more thing I wanted to tell you is just, you know, take the first product, second product. I'll tell you in there, when we are in the challenge, I'll tell you what kind of product you should select as a bonus product that will add everything value to your main product. OK, so now just select which product, which is the closest to your niche. And then let me see you in the next challenge.

Day three, we will be talking more about the final mapping. We'll have to map your funnel. OK, and here you'll understand everything, the ball. I will be clear to you what exactly you're going to offer. So I hope I hope you're excited for that. But before becoming excited, I want you to get your product ready, because that is where the entire game is changing. And I hope you from here on where you can see that, how you are going and moving ahead. So all the best for your product, Telek, the product today by now link. You know, give me in the comment box which product you selected. And we are going to make the entire game plan for you.

Funnel Mapping Challenge

Hello, everyone, I hope you are doing great, and I know that we are moving toward the day number three, challenge number three, OK, but before we go ahead, I think and I really want you to complete the earlier, you know, like challenge one challenge to if you've completed that, it is going to really help you. Okay. If not, then after finishing this one, you have to just finish up the challenge or one challenge. So these are very much linked together with each other. So I would like you to complete that first. OK, so we can go ahead. And now welcome back to this date.

Third and challenge number three. Let me take you to what is challenge number three, OK? So let me take you to the mind map of where we are at the moment. I hope you can see the mind map also. So first line number one, new selection, product selection. And then we are moving to number three, one step. Day by day, we are moving one step closer to your goal of launching your project product, you know, within nine days. And the reason behind not making this goes too dull, too long, you know, is that you launch your product in those days. OK, I do not want to give you like you're not you know, there are different coaches who are giving you the conceptual part first and then transportational parsec and the information flows and then transformationally later. But I don't want that to happen with you. OK?

I want you to complete the entire transformation in order to launch your product in the first of my calls. Yeah. It didn't help me. So let's talk about child number three. Number three is for the Stiv final mapping challenge. What is fun? Final is simply, you know, like there are different kinds of information related to the funnel. First is like, you know, how people get a word about your product and then how they consider your product and how they engage with your product and then how you don't get by the product. So this is how the sales funnel to this is kind of a sales funnel. I'm not talking about that when I'm talking about, you know, how would you sell your product?

You know, how would you sell a product and what is added to that? So you get the maximum profit out of it before moving out. Let me show you a real example of a funnel, OK? The funnel that made me million of their pieces. And, you know, when I launched this funnel, to be honest, I was so confused when I launched my product. It's called Lifetime Gunton. I've told you many times in a lifetime, continuing when I launch, Of course, it was used with the pilot product. But the problem that I had was, you know, I was very much doubtful. And if I would ever launch that product simply as the first front end product, then I wouldn't have made the money that I made. OK, I made the money because I had to add back in.

I had the second and third one time offer. Audio and audio to that is an extra offer that you add, the flavor that you add to your main Book, to your main product. And the reason behind this is I would like to thank one of my mentors. You know, you might have heard a lot about him. He's known as Richard Russell Brunson. And Russell Brunson is the one who launched this concept of funnel in the Internet marketing industry. So he had taken this idea from the Macdonald. He realized that McDonald's sells. We are actually the magnate who is not making any profit out of the burger. So the single burger, which is how much it costs you, is the cost of the customer acquisition to acquire one customer. They require that much of the cost which they are selling the burger, which they are selling the burger to you. So how do they earn profit? So they earn profit by making Chombo.

Once you go there and you don't buy the Magda's burger, they will add something extra to that. They will ask you, do you want fries and say yes, do you want Coke? Then you'll say, do you want the million Mboya combo? Back then you'll say yes. And that is how they make the entire funnel, right? That is how they make the profit. So the same concept was used by Russell Brunson in the Internet marketing industry. And later on, he also launched the click funnel that funnels a legend in our funnel making software. And that is like many of the people might know about the click funnel as well, So now here you don't have to click one. You don't have to use the click funnel. OK, I will tell you what you are to use, but I'm telling you the funnel that you have to make, and that is very, very important.

OK, so let me show you how we are going to map out the funnel. OK, what are the products that we are going to be using? So before that, I am going to show you the real example of the funnel. Yeah. My own product. Just through the second level, I am going to take you to the group. I hope you can see over here we are the chrome. And this is lifetime content being my product. And I'm really thankful to this product. You know, it was an accident. I was tired with the, you know, making the product and it was taking too much time. There was a product called Expert Budgeting Blueprint. I was making this product so I can help coaches, consultant trainers to position themselves as an expert in a particular niche. But they were taking too much of the time, so many doubts, so much reduced creation and a lot of money things, you know. And then there was no instant product.

And this product, this one, you know, this Tom Goldman was actually abseiled to my dad cause, you know, and then I didn't know what to do. And finally I launched this product. OK, whatever little information that I had, I launched this product way back in 2000. Twenty or twenty around, I think August. Yeah, around August. And you won't believe this one simple trick made me a lot of money or a year, OK? And during those times, what you saw happened, that many of my customers, my clients used to talk to me in days to ask me how you are making this product and how this is working. Very fine, Ümit. Everything is great? You know how. But are you earning anything because Facebook is not making a profit? And then I would simply, you know, ask them, why do you think Facebook is not giving?

Because I had no idea, Of course. When they start telling me how their product is not working. Then I started, you know, looking at the product, I saw everything, you know. Many of the one of my, you know, menti Azadeh Ansari, he had a product called Social Media Calendar. You're selling it to, you know, very high praise. And also there was no back and. So he was not making any money. There was one guy I remember on something called. He had a Book product which was making, you know, a good amount of money earlier, but he did not have any backend product. So in the long run, he was not making any profit out of it. And when I told him to shift and, you know, make it a funnel and all, it was already the main, you know, customer base.

Blinder's was already gone. But later on, they started making at least some money. They started making some profit out of it. This one trick that I use since the beginning of, you know, my product, that made me a lot of money. So, yeah, I'm going to show you here and I'm also going to show you two things, OK? Just how much this actually made me. I used to use RENTO. I don't use Inv. now. I used to use it a lot. So just. See, I can't. And here I'm going to show you the funnel first. OK, so you can get instant access. Yeah. So this is my front end product. OK, this is my front end product. This is a sales copy.

This lifetime content bank is my front end product. If you click over here, you're trying to buy it. OK, so the first product was for how many copies it was for the three nineties. It was around 400 rupees, OK? There's low cost. Now, when you click away here, the moment you click over here, you reach the new one time offer. That is my Ahran product. OK, that is my errant product special. One time offer. So I bundle some of the done for you, you know, content. Of course, I have worked a lot on this. And this is for 340. So and so you can add this product to your cart. So if you add this to your cart, you'll again go to my one time offer to do my second one by my point, OK? And here it is.

Upgrade your offer to get instant access to the easy way software. And this is, what, 347? So if you add this also to the cart, you'll be landing up to the combo of three packs. So you can see three nine seven three four seven three four seven one zero nine one lifetime content plus content management plus easy watch FBA. Now you may see that. Don't people get irritated about it? Yeah, Of course they do. They do get irritated, right? There is no escape from that. But um, now you will be one you will be really surprised to see what I'm going to show you or show you one more thing.

Just let me show you one more thing. OK, so when you do not let me again get back to the product. What the first product. You click here. There is no button. I'll tell you more about how to do it. OK, but there is not a word until when you click away here. You reach here. OK, here is how often you can accept this or not. Again, I made one down selldown. Like if they don't want that product, then I'll make, you know, wait. Before you go, let me give you. But especially to one of the products I'm giving them for 97 rupees only. OK, so they can say yes to this or they can say no to this if they say yes.

Let me show you no magic here. If they say yes, they'll be going here. Right, for ninety four. If they say no to this. No, I don't want them to get the first product. No. Again, I'm giving you the entire strategy here, I'm giving the entire funnel making strategy, People take a lot of money this the well, this strategy and their apostles and, you know, like the next level product. I'm going to tell you. OK, then when you add this one, just add this to my gut. Click that this is one zero nine one. If you do not add this to your cart, then click. Seven four for this first product and second audio, combined together. This is your checkout page, OK? Now, just let me show you.

Let me show you. How much lifetime content bank generated for me? Yeah. Can you see here? So this is a total of 494 customers. And again, Of course, there is a long story behind this. You know, this is, again, a product where you might not be one to one and half like rupees because Allura used to sell it on. I did not have any memberships like I just used to give them downloads. And also we had some issues. So, yeah, now I switch to the membership site, OK? And now I use better Web membership. There are a lot of problems within Rendu. I use a better membership site and I'll tell you more about it. But see the product that is for 397 that is sold over the 173 sales. OK, so 173 says 173 people have got this product.

And it had made me six to seven thousand rupees, the LC, because that is like, you know, a down -sale that only forty two people have got. But yeah, it has made me some extra. So if you sell 42 for 4200 extra rupees, It's like a Merete LCB bundle, that is seven four for 144 people. And that is what has made me want like four thousand. LCB special. That is a third product with not like all the three Bundarra three upset to upset. It's OK together with one 091 and you would be surprised to see the numbers of the conversion that is like a party at a one like 38000 I've done.

This is still the time, you know. So they like around a long back. You know, by the time you will be seeing it, the numbers would have been very different. Yeah. So but the thing I'm telling you see here, I made the sale of 173. So out of 173, 132 again, you know, so the total of around 34 to 40 people. So among the 430 people, 132 people have gone for the entire bundle. If I had only one product, I would have made the kind of profit that

I made. No, Of course not possible. I'm showing you the true figures over Yochanan.

I'm telling you the true figures. And this is April twenty. Twenty one sales picked on. OK, now and this is Jan also included. But now what I want to show you here is what wonder the sales funnel can do for you. OK, and you just need a little bit, you know, extra iBrain if you use that. See what can happen with you, OK? And that's what I'm going to tell you, that's what I'm going to teach you in the forthcoming, you know, session. So, yeah, that's what a sales funnel is all about. In the next chapter, we'll be talking about, you know, the theoretical part of the sales funnel. Let me see you in the next chapter. I hope you love this one. And if you are a miswired just right down in the comment box amidst.

Funnel Brainstorm

Welcome, everyone, once again. And now I'm going to show you a wonderful thing. OK, I know you're amazed by William, but this is the time to make your own work. You're not your mom or your own work so let me dive into the mind map over here. Will be making your sales funnel OK and or cure. You will have to do the challenge today. OK, so let's see what is in the four steps, Alisyn. The first step will be for you to step up. Why not? And don't.

What do you have? You don't have to make all the steps right now. What are the most important things that I will be doing? OK, but you should know that you should have some bird's eye view. Where are you going? The first thing is you should have a lead magnet, a lead magnet, which you will know, you can either give it for free to the people or at very minimum cost. So you might have seen people, you know, selling their WhatsApp goals or, you know, free e-book, free reports, or something like that.

Sometimes free webinar that is lead magnet. That's how they get attracted to you when you provide the value and sell them to your main product. It can be a pretty report. Short e-book equals what for you? I would suggest, you know, a free report can be a lead magnet to you, OK, where you just give the link and then they come to your main product. This can happen with the product that you have bought, the product. There will already be a limited opt in page and lead magnet given to that. OK, so that you can do it. But for now, you don't have to worry about the lead magnet coming only once your main product is ready. And the more focus has to be given to the main product, You won't believe till now I don't have a proper lead magnet for molybdenum content. Is that good? Bad.

I'm focusing on the end product. OK, so the same thing. But when you think that you're, you know, the be your sales one has to go is tied up now your sales are not coming up. And then you think about different ways to generate leads, you know, and then sell them. So right now, you don't have to think about Ohlemacher. The second is your core product. And here you have to pay more, more and more attention, OK? And the most attention that you have to pay a week here is to make your core product. So what the content model that you have got in your you know, you can check an unstoppable picking up. You can't see the entire product. See the entire world. Check it out. You'll be getting like a book.

You must have some kind of e-book checklist, resource file. If you got it from Ballarat , there might be something called an action guide audiobook you'll have to create. And I'll tell you more about it, because you'll have to create and I'll tell you more about it. Get a tutorial and the same goes for that. Yeah, same goes for the tutorial. Now Community Access is, you know, when you're offered a closed committee guide like, you know, Facebook or you can say a Facebook group, you know, you can make them in your Facebook community where you help each other, OK? So these are the things that you can do in your core product. OK, one more thing I just wanted to say. It's like a tutorial like layout tutorial.

Now, I don't know whether you're able to ceil or not. So here's just like to talk about training, lightning layout, and you'll be the better option. OK, so you give one to not one to one, but the light training to the people enrolled for your program. OK, so let's suppose that people were enrolled. So you will give all the bundles, you know, all these things about extra light training and why it is important, why it will help you, because already you have the ready-made model for you. And then you can add value with the lightning. OK, so your product gets ready. You don't have to, you know, do all the chapters at one time. You don't have to record all the chapters, OK? You just have to go to you and then, you know, take the topics and then help them out. OK, and how would you take that you will take from the book?

It's a book about making the product and refining the product. I'll tell you more about that in challenge number four, eight on a day. But on day three, we are working on the under to understand your core product. So what you have to do is first select the book, whatever book that. And Of course, there has to be some kind Of course that is given to you. Right, because when it has your name, your name on it, you know, your target is built up. So just think, you know, what can you do with this? And I want at least five minimum products that you can get. We will make it Bonos and everything. Yeah. The five products together can be combined in your main product. So you can do a book. You can do the checklist resource file. So three things.

Are there book checklists resourcefully? And if you've got your product from Peola. I'm sorry, unstoppable. You already have it. OK, audio. You can create, you know, audio books out of your book. So that is also possible. Mini Book tutorial outearning or commandeers is anything any one thing out of it? So either can give me Niko's tutorial lightning or among these three. You can. At least one. So today you can make as many calls as you can make. Or you can give labor to any, But you don't have to, you do not have to get to you to confuse Ovadia. You just have to just make whatever can be made ready, made ready for you these days. OK, so let's suppose you feel giving book checklists resourcefully. Three are done. Then let's suppose you're giving, you know, like training or 10 days later and you will be giving or, you know, 10 days weekly.

Loudonville to earn. Hofman, you will be training them weekly on the weekly basis. So that can be done and you will be getting many calls or tutorials. OK, I'll tell you how to do all that. But right now, the important point is to decide what you're going to get. What are you going to offer? OK, so bookless checklist resource file three. And then let's suppose you're giving many goals that are, Of course, OK, that are offered and community X is fine. So these are the five things that you will be giving to your in your corpora. These are the findings you will be giving to your COBRA. So that is your coprolite, the main product.

Now, you remember I told you about the funnel. Now you will have to add on to your core product. OK, so this is your front end product and not at the back end. At the back end, you need at least two otiose. That is one payment for one one dime of it. And this is the funnel, OK? In the one time offer. So when someone tries to buy your core product, you'll get many clicks on the Bible and you should be reaching over it here in the second product. Either you can give them workshop Lalai workshop.

If you are not giving a workshop in the first, then in the second you Ganguli workshop, you can give one hour, two hours for the mastermind. Or you can give complimentary abundance. So you remember I told you to buy to at least get to špidla products which are related to the industry. So another product, another product, you know, the tool kit that you can give as a bundle in order of what you want. OK, one time offer one. All you can do is get something done for you. Things like gifts of my life. I'm going to make you might have seen in the next product the bundle. You might have seen that I've given all, you know, five bundles together to the people so they can use it for them. So I'd done it for them. So do it for you. So that kind of product you can give.

The same goes for audio, too. You can do either bundle here. One thing is added is one to one class. So you can also add on Books that are done for your product or One-To-One consultation. One-To-One consultation should not be given in the audio when it should always be given on audio to And I have done this with one of my main team, Salen Sadie. And he had called it a phenomenal phenomenon, as I read the One-To-One consultation. And it was important initially because you could record those and he could, you know, show that as a case study and good and get good reviews also. And he also knew the problem pinpoints of the target market. So that can happen with you. Okay. So a cool product is like a good product consisting of fire. And then you have workshop audio on an audio to audio.

One can be like, you know, complimentary wonder and audio, too. Also can be either complimentary Mendon or any anyone ideas or either one. You don't have to do all these things together because I will tell you about how to add bonuses. You will need to add bonuses to it. OK, so bonuses are compulsories in everything. So these here are also the main product and then you will have bonuses the same way. OK, your main product and you will have bonuses. And the bonuses can be taken from the popular product itself. OK, here you are. You know, a lot of the hard work is eliminated. They are working on the main product, And you're also using psychological psychology. So that makes this wonderful. OK, so how many of you feel, you know, confident or what if you feel confident, just the right type.

Don't look confident in the comment box below, because what I'm going to tell you next is wonderful. OK, so this is your corporate lead magnet. Forget, right? Not, you know, later on you will be working on it. Just give the special report and bring them to your account and link that to the product. But in the core product that you're. And that in the back, you have audio and audio, too. And this is your level of product. Level of product means you will be scaling it up to get that. OK, you're taking it to the next level and level of product you don't have to make.

You just have to give them ideas like I have a scalar product. So once you are done with making this, you know, taking this instant longland ivied, and once you're done and you'll start making those sales, you know, then only I will pitch you the scale of the product. So now you have to scale your business to the next level. You have to make new kinds of Phiona's. And that time the scale of the product will be scalable. Lunch will be helping you. So now I'm not telling you more about it the same way. You just have to do it. And you can also generate pre-sales. And I will tell you, how can you generate peace? So can you just give a little bit idea about your product and you can do the presales you know, you can pitch in the first product only about the next product that is going to come in maybe a week or two or a month. That is the case with me. OK, so this is how I view the product. So in the lead magnet, you can have a free report, Shati book, Ecorse in the corner, like you can have a book checklist, resource.

Don't make it yourself. Don't waste your time on this, OK, because I'm going to tell you in the next 10 and how to walk on it, OK? So the book checklist is a. And in the ad on you, how you know, one workshop mastermind complimentary or due to a bundle at Uncaused done for you level of product. OK, we are presales. And then I'm going to give you the golden rule over here. See, you want to have all the answers all the time. Sometimes Journey to the Unknown starts with the correct and moving forward with the Fed. So don't if you are confused, you don't know. Just just play.

You don't take a mark on that, OK? In the core product, just take a notebook right now and make it a checklist resource for the election guide or you will get everything or just click or take on that. And then in the next challenge, you will be making things much more clearer. So, yeah, if you found this interesting. And also I would want to, you know, do one thing to you. Just go to the left of the Godalming dot deck so you can check the to the final of mine and you'll get the idea that the audio when NATO has audio has to be made. But do not get too confused. Just mark over there and will be helping you to create your and craft your product. OK, in the next challenge, tomorrow will be seeing more about adding value to your product. But for now, just draw the final draw to add on to what I want.

I can come to your mind. OK, if you. And Of course, you should be flexible for whatever extra things that are coming to your mind. You should be ready with that also. OK, with that. Remember, you don't have all the answers all the time. Sometimes the journey to the unknown is taken with faith, right? Just. Just. Don't think too much. Tomorrow will be a meeting with the next challenge today. Complete all your tasks.